THIS COMPANION BELONGS TO

_____

Illustrator: Bonnie Dain

10 9 8 7 6 5 4 3 2 1

Published by Hearst Books
A Division of Sterling Publishing Co., Inc.
387 Park Avenue South, New York, NY 10016

Town & Country and Hearst Books are trademarks of Hearst Communications, Inc.

www.townandcountrymag.com

For information about custom editions, special sales, premium and corporate
purchases, please contact Sterling Special Sales Department at 800-805-5489
or specialsales@sterlingpublishing.com.

Distributed in Canada by Sterling Publishing
c/o Canadian Manda Group, 165 Dufferin Street
Toronto, Ontario, Canada M6K 3H6

Distributed in Australia by Capricorn Link (Australia) Pty. Ltd.
P.O. Box 704, Windsor, NSW 2756 Australia

Manufactured in China

Sterling ISBN 978-1-58816-767-5

Town&Country

Travel Companion

{ **A GLOBETROTTER'S
GUIDE AND JOURNAL** }

SUSAN CRANDELL

HEARST BOOKS

A division of Sterling Publishing Co., Inc.

New York / London
www.sterlingpublishing.com

CONTENTS

FOREWORD

Probably the earliest experience any of us has ever had writing about our travels was in grade school when we were asked to compose that inevitable essay, "What I Did on My Summer Vacation." That may well have led to keeping a diary or a scrapbook based on the next family holiday—and the next, and so on. If it becomes a habit, it's not only fun to do, it can be a wonderful keepsake to be shared with subsequent generations.

Travel journalists—and I count myself as one, having edited a travel publication for many years—often take small notebooks with us and have them at the ready, day or night. I have an entire collection dating back to my first trip to Europe in 1967. It began with a trans-Atlantic crossing from New York to Naples and covered my several months of living in Italy and making side trips to as many countries I could squeeze in between. From time to time, I like to review these journals for the pure pleasure of remembering how things have changed—or, even better, how they have not.

As writing became my career, I learned to take more serious notes and now depend on them for many a major article, along with any photographs, postcards, menus and other materials I can accumulate that might jog my memory. I have lost count of the number of travel articles I've written, but I've never lost interest in keeping a record of the trip, and regard it as an instant refresher course. It also comes in handy when friends and readers ask me for restaurant recommendations, hotels to stay in, and sights to see. These days, people seem to be looking for details—a specific room number or a special table with a view; a favorite gallery in a museum, or a list of shops on a lesser-known street.

Keeping this information all in one place makes it easy to access. Of course, you could store all of the above on a computer or a BlackBerry, but there is something so much more personal about having it in a handwritten notebook.

The Town & Country Travel Companion came about as we realized just how often our readers travel and just how eager they are to jot down what they experience. So you'll find that there is plenty of room here to write about whatever strikes your fancy wherever you might be. But there's also a great deal of practical information and tips that our author, Susan Crandell, has added to make this useful and entertaining. The only thing we haven't provided is the writing instrument. That we respectfully leave up to you.

> —Pamela Fiori
> Editor in Chief
> *Town & Country*

INTRODUCTION

I can recall the exact angle of the sun as it glinted off the crests of the waves in Venice's Grand Canal, the fractured reflections of terra cotta and cream facades transforming the water into three-dimensional stained glass. I remember this image not because I'm a visual savant. Far from it. I remember because I wrote it down.

Creating a memory booster is just one of the many rewards for keeping a journal on a trip. It's not even the most important one. For my money, the best reason to take notes is because doing so transforms your experience. Becoming a journaler makes you a sponge; you touch, taste, see, and feel things with heightened attention. Shazaam. You're living in the moment, traveler's style.

I didn't discover the pleasures of keeping a travel journal until I was nearly forty and became a travel writer. Always an enthusiastic traveler, I was suddenly experiencing places with newfound vividness. Over the years, my travel journals have benefited me in many ways. Not only do my notes bring the trip rushing back in an instant, but they yield a rich harvest of recommendations—breathtaking places to go, things to see and do. If I'm lucky, they include the contact information of terrific people I've met along the way. Photographs are wonderful, but they are an erratic, episodic medium; from them, you only recall the moments of a trip they captured rather than its flow.

The trips of my life lived on either side of the great divide between when I began to keep notes and when I did not. BJ—before journal—trips were wrapped in the misty gauze of an imperfect memory. But AJ trips remain vivid in my mind because I was an active participant, really tuning into what I was doing and what was happening around me. And if the details do begin to blur, I can summon them back with a pleasurable hour spent rereading what I wrote.

You don't have to be a fabled journal writer like Charles Darwin or a world-class wordsmith like Bruce Chatwin to set phrase to page. However halting the language, it's a treat to go back and read your impressions and experiences and, perhaps, to share them with friends.

If writer's block looms, never fear. There are things you can do to make the experience sing. Number one is to regard your on-the-road musings as what they are: notes rather than a polished manuscript. Your goal is information. If you achieve verbal grace, it's a bonus. Here's the lesson that millions of bloggers have learned: just be true to yourself and set your throttle full steam ahead. You'll surprise yourself with the passion of your prose. Your job is simply to describe and explore your connection to a place.

Still drawing a blank? Consider the reporter's classic questions: who, what, where and when. Travel companions, the scene around you, even the time of day all contribute to the vibrancy of the experience.

Don't forget: a metaphor is the writer's best friend. Yes, the sky over Santa Fe is blue, but is it the vivid hue I call Popsicle blue, or the soft, soothing color of a cornflower? Does the mist sparkle as you ride a bike through the cobbled streets of Copenhagen in the early morning? Maybe the Taj Mahal reminds you of your Aunt Esther's master bath? Whatever—if that's your impression, you're entitled to it.

Don't be afraid to let others speak for you. Some of the best lines in the stories I've written have been delivered by someone other than me. I have never forgotten what another climber said on our ascent of Kilimanjaro: "an adventure is an experience where you don't know the outcome." Four years later, I still use his observation as a yardstick for life. If somebody says something funny or smart, write it down. Conversation is the life blood of novels. Let it shine in your record of events.

As the great architect Ludwig Mies van der Rohe said, "God is in the details," so don't neglect the specifics: your journal is a wonderful place to keep track of that beautiful boutique hotel in the Sixth Arrondissement or that sensational open-air barbecue joint on a Memphis backstreet—places you'll want to return to or recommend to your friends.

I like to write my notes holed up in my hotel room at the end of the day, feet up on an ottoman, sparkling water at my side. I always make sure I have a nice, fat ergonomic pen at hand to ward off cramps. Some of my friends write in their journals first thing in the morning, before they set out on the new day's adventure. Others like to sit in a coffee house; setting themselves in the middle of activity engages their muse. Either way works. The trick is in suiting your own style. I carry a tape recorder wherever I go to record impressions that might evaporate otherwise. I used to feel self-conscious speaking into it, but since the advent of cell phones, I fit right in, strolling down the street talking to myself. Then, in the evening, I transfer my impressions to paper.

There's space for seven trips in this pocketable volume, a healthy year's worth of travel, and we've spotlighted a lively assortment of destinations to inspire your trips. Some like San Francisco, Paris and Rome are classics; others, like Buenos Aires and Moscow are hot right now. Remember, as you unwind with a mojito at the end of a busy day stalking Gaudi buildings in Barcelona, the today-and-tomorrow double pleasure of keeping a journal: it both enriches your travels and insures they'll always remain fresh in your mind. Whenever I read my notes about that afternoon in Venice, I'm right back on the vaporetto, gliding along the stained-glass water of the Grand Canal.

MY LIFE LIST

Continents

- ❏ Africa
- ❏ Antarctica
- ❏ Asia
- ❏ Australia
- ❏ Europe
- ❏ North America
- ❏ South America

States

- ❏ Alabama
- ❏ Alaska
- ❏ Arizona
- ❏ Arkansas
- ❏ California
- ❏ Colorado
- ❏ Connecticut
- ❏ Delaware
- ❏ District of Columbia
- ❏ Florida
- ❏ Georgia
- ❏ Hawaii
- ❏ Idaho
- ❏ Illinois
- ❏ Indiana
- ❏ Iowa
- ❏ Kansas
- ❏ Kentucky
- ❏ Louisiana
- ❏ Maine
- ❏ Maryland
- ❏ Massachusetts
- ❏ Michigan
- ❏ Minnesota

- ❏ Mississippi
- ❏ Missouri
- ❏ Montana
- ❏ Nebraska
- ❏ Nevada
- ❏ New Hampshire
- ❏ New Jersey
- ❏ New Mexico
- ❏ New York
- ❏ North Carolina
- ❏ North Dakota
- ❏ Ohio
- ❏ Oklahoma
- ❏ Oregon
- ❏ Pennsylvania
- ❏ Rhode Island
- ❏ South Carolina
- ❏ South Dakota
- ❏ Tennessee
- ❏ Texas
- ❏ Utah
- ❏ Vermont
- ❏ Virginia
- ❏ Washington
- ❏ West Virginia
- ❏ Wisconsin
- ❏ Wyoming

My List

- ❏ _____
- ❏ _____
- ❏ _____
- ❏ _____
- ❏ _____
- ❏ _____
- ❏ _____
- ❏ _____
- ❏ _____
- ❏ _____
- ❏ _____

- ❏ _____
- ❏ _____
- ❏ _____
- ❏ _____
- ❏ _____
- ❏ _____
- ❏ _____
- ❏ _____
- ❏ _____
- ❏ _____
- ❏ _____

THE TAO OF
PACKING

Everybody has his or her own attitude about packing. Go light? Go heavy? Bring this? Leave that? Here are some suggestions on what to take and how to carry it.

Know thyself	Are you a minimalist like me, content to make do from time to time for the pleasure of traveling with carry-on only? Or do you adore being surrounded by your favorite things, and crave having a choice about what to wear each day? There's no special trick to being a big packer—just bring everything! But there's definitely an art to packing small. And as airlines levy new fees for checked bags, more travelers are becoming minimalists.
The carry-on crowd	For me, black is key to packing light; it goes with everything and can be dressed up or down. A few pieces of jewelry will do the trick. Knits and other crease-free

wonder-fabrics—brilliant. Shoes take up acres of space, so having a versatile, comfortable pair that can do double duty—walking a city by day, dining elegantly by night—is important. Don't forget that lost space inside them. I tuck my brush in one shoe, rechargers in another.

To fold or not to fold?

Our daughter is a roller, and when I saw how elegantly she packed a single oversized backpack for a nine-month round-the-world trip, I became a convert. Rolling clothing minimizes wrinkles, and makes it easy to find something without removing lots of layers. Stiff garments that won't roll can be laid on top.

Compartmentalize!

For a multi-stop trip, there's nothing like a segmented suitcase. Get used to putting your underthings in the same pocket on every trip, toiletries in one certain place and electronics in another. You'll save hours of rooting through your stuff.

And don't forget…

If you're always coming up one item short, log onto onebag.com to generate a recommended packing list by plugging in destination, typical weather, activities, gender, and such.

PACK A
TRAVEL BOOK

Pick up one of these famous travel books to take with you on the plane as inspiration.

Desert Solitaire, by Edward Abbey
Based on Abbey's time as a National Park ranger in Utah.

In Patagonia, by Bruce Chatwin
Chatwin visited in 1976, and his account remains a classic.

From Beirut to Jerusalem, by Thomas L. Friedman
A political and cultural primer on the Middle East by the New York Times Pulitzer-Prize winning writer.

Under the Tuscan Sun, by Frances Mayes
The funny, telling account of restoring a villa and making a life in sunny Italy.

Arctic Dreams, by Barry Lopez
A natural history of the far north.

Native Stranger: A Black American's Journey into the Heart of Africa, by Eddy L. Harris
Harris learnes what it means to be a Black man in the United States by traveling to another continent.

A Year in Provence, by Peter Mayle
The British adman's first book about moving to France is still his best.

The World: Travels 1950-2000, by Jan Morris
She writes about Jerusalem, Baghdad, Capetown, Kyoto and Atlanta, among other places.

Among the Believers: An Islamic Journey, by V.S. Naipaul
The Nobel-prize-winning author visits Iran, Pakistan and Malaysia.

A Short Walk in the Hindu Kush, by Eric Newby
Reflections from a mounteering expedition in northeastern Afghanistan.

In Trouble Again: A Journey Between the Orinoco and the Amazon, by Redmond O'Hanlon
Adventures in the Amazon basin.

The Great Railway Bazaar: By Train Through Asia, by Paul Theroux
One of the best-loved of Theroux's many travel titles.

SPOTLIGHT ON
SAN FRANCISCO

There's no doubt why San Francisco is one of America's favorite cities. Restaurateurs and shop owners alike just keep upping the ante on innovation. With myriad outdoor pleasures, it's a fine place for nature lovers with a city spirit.

Digs

On Nob Hill, near Union Square and Fisherman's Wharf, is the newly renovated Ritz-Carlton (ritzcarlton.com). Between the Yerba Buena cultural district and Union Square, the Four Seasons Hotel (fourseasons.com) occupies the middle floors of a skyscraper. Campton Place (tajhotels.com), on the edge of Union Square, is a boutique-hotel classic. The St. Regis Hotel, San Francisco (stregis.com/sanfrancisco) has sleek, modern lines. For incredible views, book the Mandarin Oriental, (mandarinoriental.com/sanfrancisco) in the financial district.

Eats

Eat where the locals do. At Quince, chef Michael Tusk's entrees strike an imaginative note, blending Italian and French cuisine. The atmosphere at A16, named for the autostrada that connects Naples and Bari, has delightfully authentic pizza and pasta. Cav Wine Bar & Kitchen has a flight of variations on a new theme from its fine wine collection each week. For Dungeness crab bisque or a beef fillet topped with foie gras, head for mahogany-paneled Big 4 Restaurant on Nob Hill. And don't forget Alice Waters' fabled Chez Penisse in Berkeley.

Doings

Check out the Ferry Plaza Farmer's Market on Tuesdays and Saturdays, and the fabulous de Young fine arts museum in Golden Gate Park any day but Monday. For great shopping in men's and women's clothes, drop by Wilkes Bashford on Sutter Street or Button Down on Sacramento. For antiques try Threshold by Kendall Wilkinson, Sultana, Therien & Co. and the Fraenkel Gallery.

BEST BETS FOR TRAVELING WITH KIDS

With new options for luxury and adventure, parents don't have to sacrifice refinement and kids don't have to sacrifice excitement. Here are five selections for families on the go.

Formality Plus Fun

The Winnetu Oceanside Resort, an elegant hotel on Martha's Vineyard (winnetu.com), has a kiddy-height buffet with 3D menus and an ice cream bar. There's a life-size outdoor chess set and antique cars to shuttle everyone around.

Kids' Programs Galore

Make sure activities have a breakdown by age group, there are no more than four kids per counselor, and both indoor and outdoor activities are offered. A great choice: Kids for all Seasons programs at many Four Seasons resorts (four seasons.com), including Terre Blanche

< 20 >

in Provence and Peninsula Papagayo in Costa Rica.

Suite Suites

London's Stafford Hotel (thestafford hotel.co.uk) has two-bedroom apartments fitted out for families, with free cribs and roll-away beds.

Hands-on Experience

Farm stays are a child's dream vacation. Shelburne Farms in Vermont (shel burnefarms.org) is a working farm, environmental-education center and 19th-century inn. Kids learn about sustainable agriculture while making cheese.

The Pleasures of Renting

Family-friendly villas combine hotel-level service with kids' play. Frenchmans Lookout, on Tortola in the British Virgin Islands (frenchmanslookout.com) has a playground, crib and playpen, bins of toys, plus 360-degree views of the Sir Francis Drake Channel, and the wrap-around porches have child-safe railings.

For more ideas: Consult Small World Travel, which caters to families (512-495-9495), or browse through Ciaobambino.com, which rates family-friendly villas.

Trip One

DESTINATION:

DATE:

TRAVEL COMPANIONS:

OVERALL IMPRESSIONS:

Experiences

> "*M*ost travel is best of all in the anticipation or the remembering; the reality has more to do with losing your luggage."
> —*Regina Nadelson*

> "*I* have found that there ain't no surer way to find out whether you like people or hate them than to travel with them."
>
> —*Mark Twain*

> "*L*ook deep into nature, and then you will understand everything better."
> —*Albert Einstein*

> "*In* America there are two classes of travel—first class, and with children." —*Robert Benchley*

Recommendables

HOTELS:

EATERIES:

SIGHTS:

New Friends

NAME:

ADDRESS:

PHONE:

EMAIL:

WHERE WE MET:

NAME:

ADDRESS:

PHONE:

EMAIL:

WHERE WE MET:

NAME:

ADDRESS:

PHONE:

EMAIL:

WHERE WE MET:

NAME:

ADDRESS:

PHONE:

EMAIL:

WHERE WE MET:

NAME:

ADDRESS:

PHONE:

EMAIL:

WHERE WE MET:

NAME:

ADDRESS:

PHONE:

EMAIL:

WHERE WE MET:

SPOTLIGHT ON PARIS

In the world's most romantic city, everything old is new again: century-old hotels sparkle, classic cafes shine.

Digs

For classic luxury, choose one of these venerable four: the Ritz (ritzparis.com), at the Place Vendome, Four Seasons George V (fourseasons.com), near the Champs-Elysees, the Plaza Athenee (www.plaza-athenee-paris.com) where Carrie Bradshaw swooned on a balcony, and the Meurice (lemeurice.com), near the Louvre. The Hotel du Petit Moulin (paris-hotel-petitmoulin.com), designed by Christian Lacroix in a 17th century building, does a jazzier take on elegance, near the Picasso Museum. For a trip to Versailles, the Trianon Palace and Spa (starwoodhotels.com) in a three-acre park, is the place.

Eats	Foodies flock to Alain Ducasse's new restaurant in the Eiffel Tower and Alain Senderens's restaurant on the Place de la Madeleine, called Senderens. L'Angle du Faubourg is a less costly sibling to the celebrated Taillevent. At Benoit, a well-known bistro for three generations, cassoulet is the star. Other beloved bistros include Chez L'Ami Louis, Aux Lyonnais, and Allard.
Doings	Stroll the Left Bank, and sip Pernod in a cafe with the locals, or catch the latest show at one of the city's many museums—Centre Pompidou, Musee D'Orsay, Musee Rodin. At Dessine Moi un Bijou, you can get jewelry custom-made, while Cadolle will sew you made-to-measure lingerie. On the Right Bank, American fashion designer Rick Owens has opened a boutique in the Jardins du Palais Royal. Between the Place de la Concorde and Arc de Triomphe, you'll find British designer Paul Smith, Prada, Gucci and Hermes. Parisians love the tableware at Zero One One, near the Louvre.

SAFARI MADE
SIMPLE

For most people, an African safari is a once-in-a-lifetime experience. The choices are broad: Which country? Which outfitter? What time of year? These tactics will lead you to the most rewarding trip.

To See It All	Botswana has huge herds of game and a varied landscape, from the dry brush of the Kalahari Desert to the wetlands of the Okavango Delta to the savannah of Chobe National Park. Wilderness Safaris (wilderness-safaris.com) runs twenty camps in Botswana, including lavish Mombo on an island in the Okavango; the best trips camp-hop, using a pilot/guide to transport you from place to place.
For Honeymooners	Picture the two of you alone in Africa. Jack's Camp (unchartedafrica.com) is a 1940s-style lodge set among palm trees in

< 40 >

Botswana's Makgadikgadi Salt Pans. Ten tents feature chambray cotton sheets and Persian rugs.

With the Kids

Many safari countries prohibit children under the age of ten, and tots are not encouraged. Look for small camps run by people who have children. Child-friendly Naibor (shompole.com), with nine tents in Kenya's sweeping southern Mara, even allows children under eight on request.

Sources and Resources

The right travel agent is an Africa specialist who knows the parks, migration patterns and climates of the major safari destinations, as well as the top guides. Four of the best are Marcia Gordon of F.M. Allen (fmallen.com); Maggie Maranga of Protravel International (protravelinc.com); Ellison Poe of Poe Travel (poetravel.com); and Cherri Briggs of Explore (exploreafrica.net).

Trip Two

DESTINATION:

- -

DATE:

- -

TRAVEL COMPANIONS:

- -

- -

- -

OVERALL IMPRESSIONS:

- -

- -

- -

- -

- -

- -

- -

- -

Experiences

> "*The* world is a book, and those who do not travel read only a page."
> —*Saint Augustine*

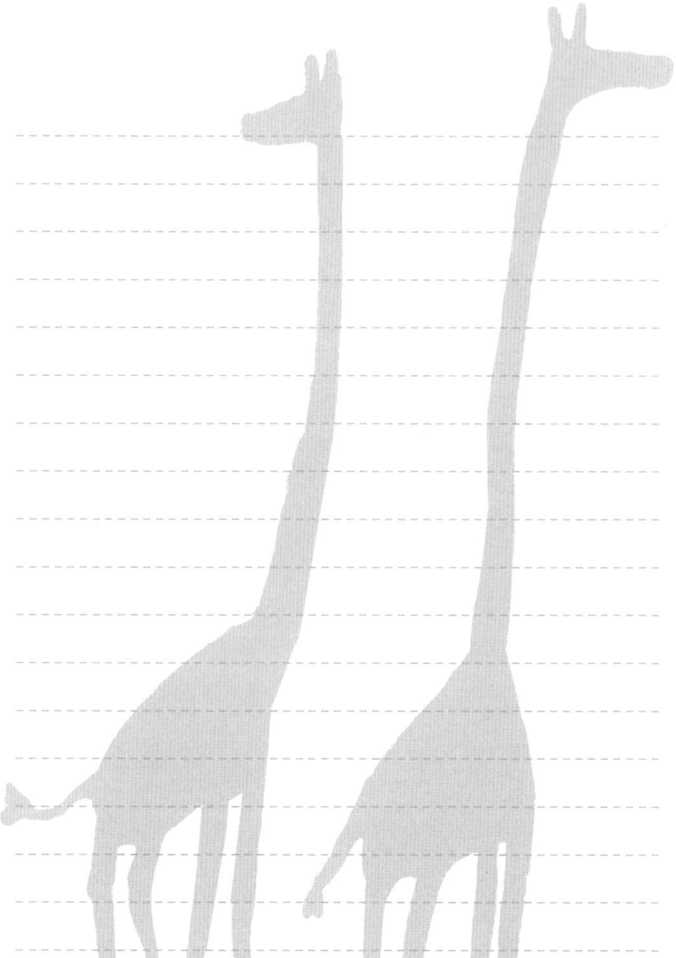

> "To get away from one's working environment is, in a sense, to get away from one's self; and this is often the chief advantage of travel and change."
>
> *—Charles Horton Cooley*

> "*The* real voyage of discovery consists not in seeking new landscapes, but in having new eyes."
> —*Marcel Proust*

> "*There are places and moments in which one is so completely alone that one sees the world entire.*"
> —*Jules Renard*

Recommendables

HOTELS:

EATERIES:

SIGHTS:

New Friends

NAME:

ADDRESS:

PHONE:

EMAIL:

WHERE WE MET:

NAME:

ADDRESS:

PHONE:

EMAIL:

WHERE WE MET:

NAME:

ADDRESS:

PHONE:

EMAIL:

WHERE WE MET:

NAME:

ADDRESS:

PHONE:

EMAIL:

WHERE WE MET:

NAME:

ADDRESS:

PHONE:

EMAIL:

WHERE WE MET:

NAME:

ADDRESS:

PHONE:

EMAIL:

WHERE WE MET:

SPOTLIGHT ON
ROME

The Eternal City is in the midst of a modern-day Renaissance. Catch the new energy of romantic Rome.

Digs

In a 16th-century building designed for Pope Julius II, the St. George Hotel (stgeorgehotel.it) is contemporary and comfortable. For every amenity you might want, there's the Hotel Eden (lemeriden.com/eden). The luxurious Hotel de Russie (hotelderussie.it) can be found between the Spanish Steps and the Piazza del Popolo. The Inn at the Roman Forum (theinnattheromanforum.com) is a well-located twelve-room hotel. Another fine boutique choice: Portrait Suites (lungarno hotels.com), on the Via Condotti.

Eats

Celebrity chef Filippo La Mantia cooks at a modern Sicilian restaurant called simply Trattoria, near the Forum. For fish, try Il

San Lorenzo, with its dark wood and contemporary art. Fresh Mediterranean cooking is the watchword at Grano, with homemade bread and pasta. The buffet at Casa Bleve is a lunchtime favorite. Aperitivo con buffet bars are migrating south to Rome; try Salotto 42, ReD, at the Auditorium Parco della Musica, or Freni e Frizioni, in Trastevere.

Doings

After drinking in the architecture from the Trevi Fountain to St. Peters to the Colosseum, you can head indoors to any number of museums. Don't miss MACRO, the Museum of Contemporary Art of Rome, or the Borghese Gallery and Museum. Then gallery-hop to Gagosian on Via Francesco Crispi, and Lorcan O'Neill on Via Orti d'Alibert. For shopping, try Soledad Twombly for one-of-a-kind clothes that are feminine and easy-to-wear (by appointment only). Lucia Odescalchi designs contemporary jewelry, using pavé diamonds, silver and gold, chain mail and mother-of-pearl. At Indoroman, you'll find hand-woven textiles from India as well as fabric home accessories crafted by Italian artisans.

HOW TO TAKE
GREAT PICTURES

Top photographers share their best tips for getting the best shots.

Know your gear

This is where the Boy Scout motto counts: be prepared. "Learn how to use your camera in advance, and bring the instruction manual with you," says Rick Sammon, author of *Rick Sammon's Complete Guide to Digital Photography 2.0.* "The people who miss shots are usually the ones fumbling with equipment."

Compose with care

"The biggest mistake? Including irrelevant features that distract from the main story," says *National Geographic* veteran Bruce Dale, who goes on to suggest moving closer, zooming in, or blocking an unattractive background with something closer to you. If the sky is overcast, leave it out.

Maximize your camera

"Take advantage of your camera's intelligence," says Ralph Lee Hopkins, who shoots for *Smithsonian*. His favorite feature is image stabilization, which can counteract camera shake. Use it to take sharp shots from a moving vehicle or for hand-held slower shutter speeds.

Go easy on the flash

"I love natural light and use a flash only when it's absolutely necessary," says Anders Overgaard, a top magazine photographer. "If you can, try one version of the shot with flash and another without." Soft lighting, under clouds or in shade, is the most flattering for people. If the light is harsh, the flash can come in handy to fill in shadows under eyes and nose.

Exercise your artistic eye

"See what makes a place special for you, like the sky at dusk reflecting in the infinity pool at your hotel," says *Town & Country* contributor Maura McEvoy. Consider creating a series of photographs with a specific theme, like close-ups of African butterflies or the market flowers in Seattle. "Have the confidence to follow your own vision."

Trip Three

DESTINATION:

DATE:

TRAVEL COMPANIONS:

OVERALL IMPRESSIONS:

Experiences

> "*A* man who has not been in Italy is always conscious of an inferiority, from his not having seen what it is expected a man should see."
> —*Samuel Johnson*

> "Everywhere I go I find a poet has been there before me."
> —Sigmund Freud

> "*O*ne cannot think well, love well, sleep well, if one has not dined well."
> —*Virginia Woolf*

> *"The airplane has unveiled for us the true face of the earth."*
> —*Antoine de Saint-Exupéry*

Recommendables

HOTELS:

_____

_____

_____

_____

_____

_____

_____

_____

_____

_____

_____

_____

EATERIES:

_____

_____

_____

_____

_____

_____

SIGHTS:

New Friends

NAME:

ADDRESS:

PHONE:

EMAIL:

WHERE WE MET:

NAME:

ADDRESS:

PHONE:

EMAIL:

WHERE WE MET:

NAME:

ADDRESS:

PHONE:

EMAIL:

WHERE WE MET:

NAME:

ADDRESS:

PHONE:

EMAIL:

WHERE WE MET:

NAME:

ADDRESS:

PHONE:

EMAIL:

WHERE WE MET:

NAME:

ADDRESS:

PHONE:

EMAIL:

WHERE WE MET:

SPOTLIGHT ON
ST. BART'S

This hilly, sun-struck French island, long a favorite of North Americans, is a true Caribbean classic.

Digs

Decision number one is whether to rent a villa or check into a resort. A sampling of offerings to help you choose: Amber House, a three-bedroom villa, has views of Corossol Bay and Gustavia; and six bedroom Bon Temps, with custom stonework and mosaics, looks over the northern coast. Both can be rented from Saint Barth V.I.P. (st-barth-vip.com). Among resorts, Hotel Saint-Barth Isle de France (isle-de-france.com) is lovely and quiet, tucked away on the eastern side of Anse (Bay) des Flamands. On the spectrum's other end is the Eden Rock (edenrockhotel.com), a lavish clutch of waterside accommodations on a promontory overlooking St. Jean Bay. Wimco (www.wimco.com) has a stunning collection of villas for rent.

Eats

In Gustavia, the classic choice is Au Port, with wonderful Creole food. Maya's serves up fresh fish and a fabulous coconut tart, right on the water in Public, on the south-western coast. For great lobster, head (not surprisingly) to La Langouste, west of the Isle de France hotel. The sushi is first-rate at Nikki Beach.

Doings

Best among the public beaches are Colombier, a two-mile hike from Baie de St. Jean or a pleasant sail; and Gouverneur or Saline, both on the island's south shore. Shoppers can buy unusual African art at Afrik'art, beach-wear at Black Swan, or Panama hats and Cuban cigars at Comptoir. For a drink, drop in at Le Select or Bar de l'Oubli, both in Gustavia, which draw a nice mix of locals and visitors.

PICKING THE
RIGHT CRUISE

As you surf websites and glossy brochures, heed these guidelines to make sure you get the ship with the chic staterooms, not the conga line.

Know thyself	What details are most important to you and your companions? For intimacy and off-the-beaten-path ports, choose a small-ship line like SeaDream or Windstar. Crave wifi? Crystal, Seabourn, Silversea and Windstar have it throughout their ships. Hate cigarette smoke? Oceania, SeaDream and Windstar prohibit smoking in cabins and most public spaces. Need space? Regent has two all-suite ships, the *Voyager* and the *Mariner*.
Get expert advice	A travel agent with cruise line expertise can make sure a ship matches your needs. How to find one? Look for a consultant

who belongs to a consortium like Virtuoso (virtuoso.com), Signature Travel Network (signaturetravelnetwork.com) or Ensemble Travel (ensembletravel.com). Use the agent to book flights; if there's a cancellation or delay, she'll help you catch up to the ship.

Consider the kids

Family cruises are so popular that the average age of passengers has dropped 13% in the last four years. Costa, Cunard and Holland America all have full-time kids' programs.

Earn frequent cruiser benefits

If you like a cruise line, stick with it to earn loyalty program rewards. Costa travelers can redeem points for shipboard discounts and advance boarding; Crystal loyalists receive cash credits; Regent offers priority restaurant and spa reservations; stay 140 nights on Seabourn and earn a free fourteen-day trip.

Don't be shy

Private bridge tour? Chocolate soufflés every night? Ask and ye shall receive. A Crystal passenger once got a suite's carpet changed to another color, just by asking nicely.

Trip Four

DESTINATION:

DATE:

TRAVEL COMPANIONS:

OVERALL IMPRESSIONS:

Experiences

> *"Architecture is frozen music."*
> *—Johann Wolfgang von Goethe*

> *"A good traveler has no fixed plans, and is not intent on arriving."*
> —*Lao Tzu*

> "*W*andering re-establishes the original harmony which once existed between man and the universe."
> —*Anatole France*

> "*Travel and change of place impart new vigor to the mind.*"
> —*Seneca*

Recommendables

HOTELS:

- -

- -

- -

- -

- -

- -

- -

- -

- -

- -

- -

EATERIES:

- -

- -

- -

- -

- -

SIGHTS:

New Friends

NAME:

ADDRESS:

PHONE:

EMAIL:

WHERE WE MET:

NAME:

ADDRESS:

PHONE:

EMAIL:

WHERE WE MET:

NAME:

ADDRESS:

PHONE:

EMAIL:

WHERE WE MET:

NAME:

ADDRESS:

PHONE:

EMAIL:

WHERE WE MET:

NAME:

ADDRESS:

PHONE:

EMAIL:

WHERE WE MET:

NAME:

ADDRESS:

PHONE:

EMAIL:

WHERE WE MET:

SPOTLIGHT ON
BUENOS AIRES

After its country's economic free fall in 2002, this beautiful South American city has rebounded with gusto. Bonus points: the local shopping is still a bargain.

Digs

There's marble and gold leaf galore at the Alvear Palace (alvearpalace.com), one of BA's most revered hotels. The nearby Four Seasons Buenos Aires (fourseasons.com) has a handsome outdoor pool. The new kid is town is the Palacio Duhau-Park Hyatt Buenos Aires (buenosaires.park. hyatt.com), with a spa in a 1930s mansion. The hippest choice is Faena Hotel & Universe (faenahoteland universe.com), with a theatrical crowd and a cabaret, in Puerto Madero.

Eats

For crepes and quiche, head to Brasserie Petanque, popular with Europeans. The city's best-known (and most expensive) steak house is Cabana Las Lilas. A cozy option for couples is Social Paraiso in Palermo. For riverside dining, try Patagonia Sur.

Doings

Tango lessons should be on every visitor's dance card. Avoid the many cafes in La Boca and San Telmo that advertise walk-in lessons. Instead check the listings in whatsupbuenosaires.com. Inspiring stops: La Casa Rosada, the massive pink palace of the Perons, where Madonna was filmed singing "Don't Cry for Me Argentina," the recently renovated Teatro Colon opera house and La Recoleta cemetery, with its Greek neo-classical architecture. In Recoleta, the classic shopping district, Cat Ballou has silk and satin gowns, Evangelina Bomparola sells beaded sweaters and silk dresses, and Tramando stocks clothing, shoes and accessories. For leather, try Calle Florida, touristy but full of good finds. When it's time to unwind with a cocktail, a great place to see and be seen is Casa Cruz, with its plush velvet couches. Or head for Sucre, for one of B.A.'s trendiest scenes.

SURVIVING A
LONG FLIGHT

In these days of overcrowded terminals and airplanes, delayed and cancelled flights, arriving fresh at the end of a long journey requires a careful plan.

Prepare mentally

Adjust to the time at your destination when you board a flight; reset your watch, and time your eating and sleeping, as best you can, to the rhythms of your destination.

Savor the small comforts

Fly first class or business class if you can, wear your most comfortable clothing, don noise-canceling earphones and don't forget your iPod.

Hydrate your body, inside and out

You become dehydrated more quickly at altitude (airliner cabins are pressurized to about 8,000 feet), so be sure to drink lots and lots of water. Rehydrate your skin, too, with a good moisturizer.

Avoid drugs and alcohol	Tempting as it is to pop an Ambien or sip a few glasses of Cabernet, go natural for semi-long flights. If possible, book a late evening flight, so you can sleep on board without aids. However, for an extremely long flight, one Ambien—and no alcohol—will help you arrive refreshed.
Eat lightly or not at all	Flying at altitude can strain your digestive system, so lighten up on meals. Some fliers even fast on shorter flights.
Exercise	You want to keep your blood flowing to prevent clots, so get up and move around every few hours. Do leg lifts in your seat, or simple stretches in the aisle.
Adjust to the local time	Upon arrival, set a schedule at your destination and keep to it, such as working out before breakfast each day. Try not to nap, which will only confuse your internal clock.
Book an airline with good long-haul amenities	Several airlines supply cotton sleep wear in first class. Some, including Japan Airlines, Cathay Pacific, Singapore Airlines, Alaska Airlines and American Airlines offer internet access onboard.

Trip Five

DESTINATION:

DATE:

TRAVEL COMPANIONS:

OVERALL IMPRESSIONS:

Experiences

> "One learns first of all in beach living the art of shedding; how little one can get along with, not how much."
> —*Anne Morrow Lindbergh*

> "*I*'ve known rivers ancient as the world and older than the flow of human blood in human veins. My soul has grown deep like the rivers."
> —*Langston Hughes*

> "*The* richness I achieve comes from nature, the source of my inspiration."
> —*Claude Monet*

> "*Do* not go where the path may lead, go instead where there is no path and leave a trail."
> —*Ralph Waldo Emerson*

Recommendables

HOTELS:

EATERIES:

SIGHTS:

New Friends

NAME: --

ADDRESS: --

PHONE: --

EMAIL: --

WHERE WE MET: --

NAME: --

ADDRESS: --

PHONE: --

EMAIL: --

WHERE WE MET: --

NAME: --

ADDRESS: --

PHONE: --

EMAIL: --

WHERE WE MET: --

NAME:

ADDRESS:

PHONE:

EMAIL:

WHERE WE MET:

NAME:

ADDRESS:

PHONE:

EMAIL:

WHERE WE MET:

NAME:

ADDRESS:

PHONE:

EMAIL:

WHERE WE MET:

SPOTLIGHT ON
MOSCOW

The city is evolving at lightning speed, and the stark Soviet landscape is giving way to over-the-top restaurants, flashy nightclubs and cutting-edge fashion.

Getting Around

The easiest way to navigate the city is to hire a driver or tour guide. Exeter International (exeterinternational.com) can book one in advance, and get you exclusive Kremlin visits. But don't be afraid to hop the Metro, an easy way to get around town. If Cyrillic characters are unfamiliar, memorize the overall look of the name of the stop you want.

Digs

Across the street from Red Square, the Ritz-Carlton Moscow (ritzcarlton.com) is a glitzy addition to the city's growing list of luxury accommodations. For understated chic, check into the Ararat Park Hyatt Moscow (Moscow.park.hyatt.com), or have a vodka at the rooftop bar. With just eighty-four suites, MaMaison Pokrovka (pokrovka-moscow.com), in northern Moscow, avoids the bustle and traffic of Red Square.

Eats

Café Pushkin is a classic, offering a family-style menu of traditional Russian and French dishes. A Baroque-inspired palace with chinoiserie accents is the setting at Turandot. For a authentic dinner, try Beloye Solntse Pustyni, which serves Uzbek cuisine in front of an artificial waterfall and nightly belly dancing.

Doings

The sprawling State Tretyakov Gallery exhibits only Russian art (a must for first-timers), while the Pushkin Museum of Fine Arts has an international collection. For contemporary art, drop into the Aidan Gallery in Vinzavod, or the PROUN Gallery, which curates shows that focus on Russia's past. The stylish TsUM is where Muscovite society women leaf through racks of Miu Miu and Valentino, while Cara & Co. sells clothing by cult labels from Belgium and elsewhere. Solo de Marco is a popular lounge where Russians take their karaoke seriously.

MINIMIZING MEDICAL RISKS

Even the savviest travelers neglect to plan for health emergencies overseas. An ounce of prevention can deliver a pound of cure on a far-flung trip.

Check your health plan

Consider purchasing travel health insurance. Special travel coverage providers are listed on the U.S. Department of State's Web site (www.state.gov). Some policies are sold per trip, others on an annual basis. Most are supplemental, which means they pay over and above what your own health plan pays. When choosing, ask about dollar limits on the cost of emergency care. Are translators included? What are the policy's exclusions, such as preexisting conditions and pregnancy?

Carry a medikit

Bring first aid supplies (prepackaged versions are sold at drugstores) including antihistamines and decongestants; pain and fever meds such as Tylenol; antacids; a mild laxative and an antidiarrheal drug; a cough suppressant; antifungal and anti-bacterial ointments; 1% cortisone cream; plus bandages, gauze, antibacterial hand wipes, tweezers and a thermometer. If you bring prescription medications keep them in the original bottle with pharmacy label, and carry a copy of the prescription. Ask your doctor whether to bring Cipro or another antibiotic. Finally, carry a brief summary of your medical history (chronic illnesses, allergies, blood type, drugs you take) as well as a list of the inoculations you've had and the phone number or e-mail of your primary physician. (Remember to pack the med-kit in checked luggage if it includes items you can't carry on, but keep with you any pre-scription medications you need.)

Know whom to call

Before you go, print out the addresses and phone numbers of government facilities, such as embassies and consulates, that can help you. Your travel health insurer should be the first call, but in a pinch you can turn to your credit-card company. Many provide free international referral services for medical professionals and hospitals.

Trip Six

DESTINATION:

DATE:

TRAVEL COMPANIONS:

OVERALL IMPRESSIONS:

Experiences

> "When preparing to travel, lay out all your clothes and all your money. Then take half your clothes and twice the money."
> —Susan Heller

> "*The* traveler was active; he went strenuously in search of people, of adventure, of experience. The tourist is passive; he expects interesting things to happen to him."
>
> —*Daniel J. Boorstin*

> "*Autumn* burned brightly, a running flame through the mountains, a torch flung to the trees."
> —*Faith Baldwin*

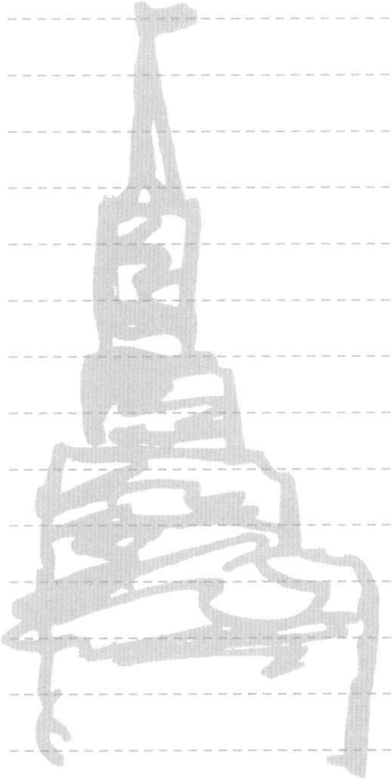

> "*L*ike all great travelers, I have seen more than I can remember, and remember more than I have seen."
> —*Benjamin Disraeli*

Recommendables

HOTELS:

_____

_____

_____

_____

_____

_____

_____

_____

_____

_____

_____

_____

_____

EATERIES:

_____

_____

_____

_____

_____

_____

SIGHTS:

New Friends

NAME:

ADDRESS:

PHONE:

EMAIL:

WHERE WE MET:

NAME:

ADDRESS:

PHONE:

EMAIL:

WHERE WE MET:

NAME:

ADDRESS:

PHONE:

EMAIL:

WHERE WE MET:

NAME:

ADDRESS:

PHONE:

EMAIL:

WHERE WE MET:

NAME:

ADDRESS:

PHONE:

EMAIL:

WHERE WE MET:

NAME:

ADDRESS:

PHONE:

EMAIL:

WHERE WE MET:

SPOTLIGHT ON SHANGHAI

Trendy and exciting, this fabled Chinese city sizzles with chic hotels, handsome colonial sites, skyscraper hotels and fabulous food.

Digs

Check into the Grand Hyatt Shanghai (shanghai.grand.hyatt.com) in the Pudong business district for stunning city views. The Portman Ritz-Carlton (ritzcarlton.com) and the Four Seasons (fourseasons.com) are elegant, efficient and well-located downtown. The Peace Hotel (shanghaipeacehotel.com) has a historic Art Deco design, and the popular Old Jazz Bar. 88 Xintiandi (88xintiandi.com) is Shanghai's first boutique hotel.

Eats

Shanghai restaurants deliver a comprehensive gastronomic tour of China. Xin Jishi, in the Xintiandi neighborhood, serves all the area specialties—doumiano (sautéed pea shoots), cong you ban (noodles seasoned with scallions), and xia ren (shrimp stir-fried with rice wine). Di Shui Dong, on Maoming Road, has great Hunan food; for Sichuan, try the Sichuan Court in the Hilton Hotel. Travelers in the know head to Wang Jia Sha, a hole in the wall on Nanjing Road with dumplings loved by the locals.

Doings

Walk the Bund to see the colonial buildings along the Huangpu River. On Nanjing Road, the premier shopping street, you'll find Tiffany, Louis Vuitton, Hermes and Chanel. For local designers, head to Tsai Mont-Hsia Couture on Maoming Road. Don't miss Dongjiadu, the city's huge fabric market, where they'll whip up a perfect garment for you in a few days. Just north of the Bund, explore traditional neighborhoods that are fast disappearing.

HOW TO GO SOLO

Many people find traveling alone off-putting or down-right scary. It needn't be. Here's how to make your next trip safe, comfortable and rewarding.

Do your paperwork	Be sure to leave a detailed itinerary and photocopy of your passport with a relative or friend back home. Then scan your passport, any visas and airline tickets and e-mail them to yourself. In an emergency, you can print them out at a cybercafe.
Pack smart	Keep your load light, so you won't have to manage an unwieldy collection of luggage, and manageable, with a simple, wrinkle-free color-coordinated wardrobe.
Choose hotels with care	Look for amenities that make single travelers feel welcome, like a door with dead bolt and peephole or valet parking (so you don't have to search for your rental car in

a dark garage), and a neighborhood that's well lighted and bustling at night.

Play it safe

Carry a cell phone that works abroad and leave flashy clothes and jewelry, which can attract unwanted attention, at home. Observe local customs regarding dress; the U.S. Department of State's Bureau of Consular Affairs (travel.state.gov) has a brochure for women traveling alone.

Hire some help

In a foreign country where you don't know the language, consider booking a driver and/or a guide. If you do drive yourself, make sure your vehicle has a navigation system.

Buy single tickets

Don't hesitate to buy one seat for the opera, a concert or the theater. You'll make friends with the people sitting around you. You can go on arranged trips focused on art or music, such as through On Tour (goontour.com), which arranges cultural excursions.

Cruise the web

There are a number of websites for solo travelers, including Travelaloneandlove it.com and the Women's Travel Club (womenstravelclub.com).

Trip Seven

DESTINATION:
_____

DATE:
_____

TRAVEL COMPANIONS:
_____
_____
_____
_____

OVERALL IMPRESSIONS:
_____
_____
_____
_____
_____
_____
_____
_____
_____

Experiences

> "*Food* is
> our common
> ground, a universal
> experience."
> —*James Beard*

> "When you're traveling, you are what you are right there and then. People don't have your past to hold against you. No yesterdays on the road."
> —*William Least Heat-Moon*

< 148 >

> *"If* you reject the food, ignore the customs, fear the religion and avoid the people, you might better stay home."
>
> —*James Michener*

> "*If* God had really intended men to fly, he'd make it easier to get to the airport."
> —*George Winters*

Recommendables

HOTELS:

EATERIES:

SIGHTS:

New Friends

NAME:

ADDRESS:

PHONE:

EMAIL:

WHERE WE MET:

NAME:

ADDRESS:

PHONE:

EMAIL:

WHERE WE MET:

NAME:

ADDRESS:

PHONE:

EMAIL:

WHERE WE MET:

NAME:

ADDRESS:

PHONE:

EMAIL:

WHERE WE MET:

NAME:

ADDRESS:

PHONE:

EMAIL:

WHERE WE MET:

NAME:

ADDRESS:

PHONE:

EMAIL:

WHERE WE MET:

WEBSITES

Town&Country offers expert advice and tips on shopping, travel fashion, travel insurance and more: townandcountrymag.com

Airport Security Info for the latest on carry-on restrictions, watch lists, etc.: tsa.gov

Airplane Seating Charts: seatguru.com

Flight Status: flightstatus.com

State Department (passport and visa requirements, registration with embassies): travel.state.gov

Travel Health (malaria areas, vaccination clinics, other info worldwide from the Centers for Disease Control): cdc.gov/travel

Emergency Services (members receive medical consultations abroad, transportation and evacuation): globalrescue.com

Exchange Rates (global currency evaluations in real time): oanda.com

Luggage Shipping: luggageforward.com

International Cellphones (buy or rent): roadpost.com

Embassy Finder: embassyworld.com

ATM Finders
American Express: amex.via.infonow.net/locator/cash/
MasterCard:
mastercard.com/us/personal/en/cardhnolderservices/atmlocations/
Visa: visa.via.infonow.net/locator/global/jsp/searchpage.jps

TIME ZONE MAP

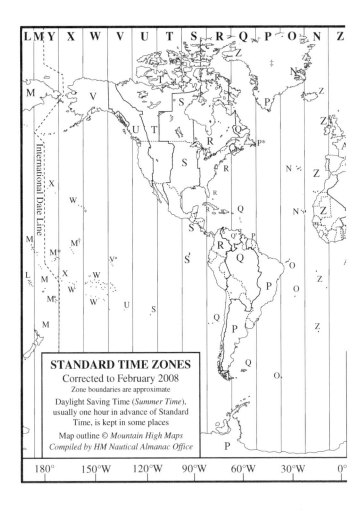

LM Y X W V U T S R Q P O N Z

International Date Line

STANDARD TIME ZONES

Corrected to February 2008

Zone boundaries are approximate

Daylight Saving Time (*Summer Time*),
usually one hour in advance of Standard
Time, is kept in some places

Map outline © *Mountain High Maps*
Compiled by HM Nautical Almanac Office

180°   150°W   120°W   90°W   60°W   30°W   0°

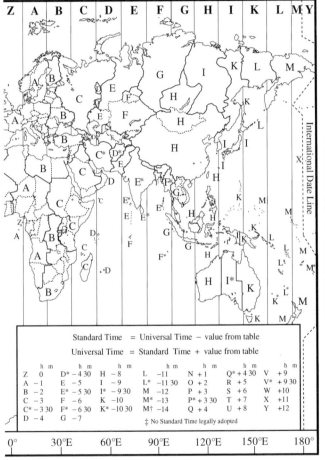

WORLD MAP OF TIME ZONES

International Date Line

Standard Time = Universal Time − value from table

Universal Time = Standard Time + value from table

	h m		h m		h m		h m		h m		h m		h m
Z	0	D*	− 4 30	H	− 8	L	−11	N	+ 1	Q*	+ 4 30	V	+ 9
A	− 1	E	− 5	I	− 9	L*	−11 30	O	+ 2	R	+ 5	V*	+ 9 30
B	− 2	E*	− 5 30	I*	− 9 30	M	−12	P	+ 3	S	+ 6	W	+10
C	− 3	F	− 6	K	−10	M*	−13	P*	+ 3 30	T	+ 7	X	+11
C*	− 3 30	F*	− 6 30	K*	−10 30	M†	−14	Q	+ 4	U	+ 8	Y	+12
D	− 4	G	− 7										

‡ No Standard Time legally adopted

0° 30°E 60°E 90°E 120°E 150°E 180°

INTERNATIONAL SIZE CONVERSIONS

Women's Clothing

USA	0/ XS	2/ XS	4/ XS	6/S	8/S	10/M	12/M	14/L	16/L	18/ XL	20/ XL
EUR	30	32	34	36	38	40	42	44	46	48	50
UK	4	6	8	10	12	14	16	18	20	22	24

Women's Shoes

USA	5	5-1/2	6	6-1/2	7	7-1/2	8	8-1/2	9	9-1/2	10
EUR	35	35-1/2	36	37	37-1/2	38	38-1/2	39	40	41	42
UK	2-1/2	3	3-1/2	4	4-1/2	5	5-1/2	6	6-1/2	7	7-1/2

Men's Clothing

USA	34	36	38	40	42	44	46	48	50
EUR	44	46	48	50	52	54	56	58	60
UK	34	36	38	40	42	44	46	48	50

Men's Shoes

USA	6	6-1/2	7	7-1/2	8	8-1/2	9	9-1/2	10
EUR	38	39	40	41	42	43	44	45	46
UK	5-1/2	6	6-1/2	7	7-1/2	8	8-1/2	9	9-1/2

CONVERSION CHARTS

Meters to Feet/ Feet to Meters

METERS	FEET
1	3.28
10	32.80
50	164.04
100	328.0

FEET	METERS
1	0.30
10	3.04
50	15.24
100	30.4

Gallons to Liters/Liters to Gallons

GALLONS	LITERS
1	3.76
5	18.92
25	94.63
50	189.27

LITERS	GALLONS
1	0.26
5	1.32
25	6.60
50	13.20

Kilograms to Pounds/Pounds to Kilograms

KILOGRAMS	POUNDS	POUNDS	KILOGRAMS
1	2.20	1	0.45
10	22.04	10	4.53
50	110.23	50	22.67
75	165.34	75	34.01
100	220.4	100	45.3

Kilometers to Miles/Miles to Kilometers

KILOMETERS	MILES	MILES	KILOMETERS
1	0.62	1	1.60
5	3.10	5	8.04
10	6.21	10	16.09
25	15.53	25	40.23
50	31.06	50	80.46
100	62.1	100	160/9

Fahrenheit to Celsius

F	C	F	C	F	C	F	C	F	C	F	C
100	37.7	81	27.2	62	16.7	43	6.1	24	-4.4	5	-15
99	37.2	80	26.6	61	16.1	42	5.6	23	-5	4	-15.5
98	36.6	79	26.1	60	15.5	41	5	22	-5.6	3	-16.1
97	36.1	78	25.5	59	15	40	4.4	21	-6.1	2	-16.7
96	35.5	77	25	58	14.4	39	3.9	20	-6.7	1	-17.2
95	35	76	24.4	57	13.9	38	3.3	19	-7.2	0	-17.8
94	34.4	75	23.9	56	13.3	37	2.8	18	-7.8	-1	-18.3
93	33.9	74	23.3	55	12.8	36	2.2	17	-8.3	-2	-18.9
92	33.3	73	22.8	54	12.2	35	1.7	16	-8.9	-3	-19.4
91	32.7	72	22.2	53	11.7	34	1.1	15	-9.4	-4	-20
90	32.2	71	21.6	52	11.1	33	.06	14	-10	-5	-20.5
89	31.6	70	21.1	51	10.5	32	0	13	-10.5	-6	-21.1
88	31.1	69	20.5	50	10	31	-.06	12	-11.1	-7	-21.6
87	30.5	68	20	49	9.4	30	-1.1	11	-11.7	-8	-22.2
86	30	67	19.4	48	8.9	29	-1.7	10	-12.2	-9	-22.8
85	29.4	66	18.9	47	8.3	28	-2.2	9	-12.8	-10	-23.3
84	28.9	65	18.3	46	7.8	27	-2.7	8	-13.3		
83	28.3	64	17.8	45	7.2	26	-3.3	7	-13.8		
82	27.8	63	17.2	44	6.7	25	-3.9	6	-14.4		

INTERNATIONAL DIALING CODES

Country Code (CC)
The Country Code is the prefix that is used when phoning to a country from another country.

International Direct Dialing Prefix (IDD)
The International Direct Dialing prefix (IDD) is the prefix needed to make a call from a country to another country. You will usually also have to provide the country code for the country you are calling. In other words, you will dial: IDD – CC – area code – phone number.

Note: If you are calling to countries or territories that use the same country code as the country you are calling from, you will not need to use the IDD prefix. Countries you may dial from the United States are marked with an asterisk.

Country	IDD	CC
Afghanistan	00	93
Albania	00	355
Algeria	00	213
American Samoa	00	684
Andorra	00	376
Angola	00	244

Country	IDD	CC
Anguilla	011	264*
Antarctica		672
Antigua	011	268*
Argentina	00	54
Armenia	00	374
Aruba	00	297

Country	IDD	CC
Ascension Island	00	247
Australia	0011	61
Austria	00	43
Azberbaijan	00	994
Bahamas	011	242*
Bahrain	00	973

Country	IDD	CC
Bangladesh	00	880
Barbados	011	246*
Barbuda	011	268*
Belarus	8~10	375
Belgium	00	32
Belize	00	501
Benin	00	229
Bermuda	011	441*
Bhutan	00	975
Bolivia	00	591
Bosnia	00	387
Botswana	00	267
Brazil	00	55
British Virgin Islands	011	284*
Brunei	00	673
Bulgaria	00	359
Burkina Faso	00	226
Burma (Myanmar)	00	95
Burundi	00	257
Cambodia	001	855
Cameroon	00	237
Canada	011	1
Cape Verde Islands	0	238
Cayman Islands	011	345*

Country	IDD	CC
Central African Rep.	00	236
Chad	15	235
Chile	00	56
China	00	86
Christmas Island	0011	61
Cocos Islands	0011	61
Colombia	00	57
Comoros	00	269
Congo	00	242
Congo, Dem. Rep. of	00	243
Cook Islands	00	682
Costa Rica	00	506
Croatia	00	385
Cuba	119	53
Cyprus	00	357
Czech Republic	00	420
Denmark	00	45
Diego Garcia	00	246
Djibouti	00	253
Dominica	011	767*
Dominican Rep.	011	809*
Ecuador	00	593
Egypt	00	20
El Salvador	00	503

Country	IDD	CC
Equatorial Guinea	00	240
Eritrea	00	291
Estonia	00	372
Ethiopia	00	251
Faeroe Islands	00	298
Falkland Islands	00	500
Fiji Islands	00	679
Finland	00	358
France	00	33
French Antilles	00	596
French Guiana	00	594
French Polynesia	00	689
Gabon	00	241
Gambia	00	220
Georgia	8~10	995
Germany	00	49
Ghana	00	233
Gibraltar	00	350
Greece	00	30
Greenland	00	299
Grenada	011	473*
Guadeloupe	00	590
Guam	011	671*

Country	IDD	CC
Guantanamo Bay	00	5399
Guatemala	00	502
Guinea	00	224
Guinea Bissau	00	245
Guyana	001	592
Haiti	00	509
Honduras	00	504
Hong Kong	001	852
Hungary	00	36
Iceland	00	354
India	00	91
Indonesia	001/ 008	62
Iran	00	98
Iraq	00	964
Ireland	00	353
Israel	00	972
Italy	00	39
Ivory Coast	00	225
Jamaica	011	876*
Japan	001	81
Jordan	00	962
Kazakhstan	8~10	7
Kenya	000	254
Kiribati	00	686
Korea, North	00	850
Korea, South	001	82

Country	IDD	CC
Kuwait	00	965
Kyrgyzstan	00	996
Laos	00	856
Latvia	00	371
Lebanon	00	961
Lesotho	00	266
Liberia	00	231
Libya	00	218
Liechtenstein	00	423
Lithuania	00	370
Luxembourg	00	352
Macau	00	853
Macedonia	00	389
Madagascar	00	261
Malawi	00	265
Malaysia	00	60
Maldives	00	960
Mali	00	223
Malta	00	356
Mariana Islands	011	670*
Marshall Islands	011	692
Martinique	00	596
Mauritania	00	222
Mauritius	00	230
Mayotte Islands	00	269
Mexico	00	52

Country	IDD	CC
Micronesia	011	691
Midway Island	011	808*
Moldova	00	373
Monaco	00	377
Mongolia	001	976
Montserrat	011	664*
Morocco	00	212
Mozambique	00	258
Myanmar (Burma)	00	95
Namibia	00	264
Nauru	00	674
Nepal	00	977
Netherlands	00	31
Netherlands Antilles	00	599
Nevis	011	869*
New Caledonia	00	687
New Zealand	00	64
Nicaragua	00	505
Niger	00	227
Nigeria	009	234
Niue	00	683
Norfolk Island	00	672
Norway	00	47
Oman	00	968

Country	IDD	CC
Pakistan	00	92
Palau	011	680
Palestine	00	970
Panama	00	507
Papua New Guinea	05	675
Paraguay	002	595
Peru	00	51
Philippines	00	63
Poland	00	48
Portugal	00	351
Puerto Rico	011	787*/ 939*
Qatar	00	974
Reunion Island	00	262
Romania	00	40
Russia	8~10	7
Rwanda	00	250
St. Helena	00	290
St. Kitts	011	869*
St. Lucia	011	758*
St. Perre & Miquelon	00	508
St. Vincent	011	784*
San Marino	00	378
Sao Tome & Principe	00	239
Saudi Arabia	00	966

Country	IDD	CC
Senegal	00	221
Serbia	99	381
Seychelles	00	248
Sierra Leone	00	232
Singapore	001	65
Slovakia	00	421
Slovenia	00	386
Solomon Islands	00	677
Somalia	00	252
South Africa	09	27
Spain	00	34
Sri Lanka	00	94
Sudan	00	249
Suriname	00	597
Swaziland	00	268
Sweden	00	46
Switzerland	00	41
Syria	00	963
Taiwan	002	886
Tajikistan	8~10	992
Tanzania	00	255
Thailand	001	66
Togo	00	228
Tonga	00	676
Trinidad & Tobago	011	868*
Tunisia	00	216
Turkey	00	90

Country	IDD	CC
Turkmenistan	8~10	993
Turks & Caicos	011	649*
Tuvalu	00	688
Uganda	000	256
Ukraine	8~10	380
United Arab Emirates	00	971
United Kingdom	00	44
Uruguay	00	598
USA	011	1
US Virgin Islands	011	340*
Uzbekistan	8~10	998
Vanuatu	00	678
Vatican City	00	39
Venezuela	00	58
Vietnam	00	84
Wake Island	00	808
Wallis & Futuna	19~	681
Western Samoa	00	685
Yemen	00	967
Yugoslavia	99	381
Zambia	00	260
Zimbabwe	00	263

MINI-TRANSLATION GUIDE

These terms will come in handy—in any country.

Hello

French	Bonjour
German	Guten Tag
Italian	Ciao
Japanese	Konnichiwa
(Mandarin) Chinese	Ni Hao
*Russian	Zdravstvujte
Spanish	Buenas Dias
Swahili	Hujambo

How are you?

Chinese	Ni Hao Ma?
French	Comment allez vous?
German	Wie geht es Ihnen?
Italian	Come sta?

How are you? *(continued)*

Japanese	O genki desu ka?
*Russian	Kak vy pozhivaete?
Spanish	Como estas?
Swahili	Habari yako?

Excuse me.

Chinese	Qingwen.
French	Excusez-moi!
German	Entschuldigen Sie!
Italian	Scusi!
Japanese	Sumimasen.
*Russian	Izvinite.
Spanish	Perdon!
Swahili	Samahani.

How much does this cost?

Chinese	Zhege duoshao qian?
French	C'est combien?
German	Wieviel kosstet das?
Italian	Quanto costa?
Japanese	Ikura desu ka?
Russian	Skol'ko eto stoit?
Spanish	Cuanto cuesta?
Swahili	Hii ni bei gani?

Thank you.

Chinese	Xiexie
French	Merci
German	Danke
Italian	Grazie
Japanese	Domo
Russian	Spasibo.
Spanish	Gracias
Swahili	Asante sana

Where's the toilet?

Chinese	Cesuo zai nail?
French	Ou sont les toilettes?
German	Wo ist die Toilette?
Italian	Dov'e la toilette?
Japanese	Benjo wa doko desu ka?
Russian	Izvinite, gde tualet?
Spanish	Donde estan los aseos?
Swahili	Choo kiko wapi?

I don't understand.

Chinese	Wo tingbudong.
French	Je ne comprends pas.
German	Ich verstehe nicht.
Italian	No capisco.
Japanese	Wakarimasen.
Russian	Ja ne ponimaju.
Spanish	No entiendo.
Swahili	Sifahamu.

* Russian and Chinese are spelled phonetically.

How do I get to _____?

Chinese	Zenme qu_____?
French	Ou se trouve _____?
German	Wie komme ich zur _____?
Japanese	_____wa dochira desu ka?
Italian	Come di arriva a _____?
*Russian	Izvinite, ja pravil'no idu k _____?
Spanish	¿Como puedo llegar a _____?
Swahili	Unaweza kunionyesha _____? (note that this is literally, Can you show me the_____?)

*Russian and Chinese are spelled phonetically.

INDEX